The Revenge of Rumpelstiltskin

A Math Adventure

by Pam Calvert

illustrated by Wayne Geehan

ini Charlesbridge

To my helper, my husband Rex, and my 2 x 2 children, Kayla, Holly, Rhett, and Courtney. Multiply them by infinity = my love! — P. C.

To my cousin up north, Sandy, her husband Jason, and daughter Nicholle. — W. G.

Published by Charlesbridge, 85 Main Street, Watertown, MA 02472
(617) 926-0329 • www.charlesbridge.com

Library of Congress Cataloging-in-Publication Data
Calvert, Pam, 1966-
 Multiplying menace : the revenge of Rumpelstiltskin / by Pam Calvert ; illustrated by Wayne Geehan.
  p. cm.
 Summary: Ten years after being tricked, Rumpelstiltskin returns to the royal family to wreak vengeance using multiplication. Includes nonfiction math notes about multiplying by whole numbers and by fractions.
 ISBN 978-1-57091-889-6 (reinforced for library use)
 ISBN 978-1-57091-890-2 (softcover)
 ISBN 978-1-60734-156-7 (ebook pdf)
 [1. Multiplication—Fiction. 2. Characters in literature—Fiction.] I. Geehan, Wayne, ill. II. Title.
PZ7.C138Mu 2005
 [Fic]—dc22   2004023072

Printed by Sung In Printing
in Gunpo-Si, Kyonggi-Do, Korea

(hc) 10 9 8 7 6 5 4 3 2 1
(sc) 15 14

The castle was full of guests celebrating Peter's tenth birthday.

"You have one gift left," said his mother, the Queen.
A big bouncy puppy ran out and licked Peter's face.

"This is the best birthday ever," Peter said as he ran his
fingers over the dog's soft fur. Just then, down the stairs
came a thunderous rumbling and a cloud of smoke.

Peter watched as the smoke cleared. There stood a strange little man who said to him in a high, squeaky voice, "I have come for you."

"Go away!" the Queen gasped. "I said your name ten years ago, and I will say it again. Rumpelstiltskin!"

"You can't get rid of me so easily this time. Ten years ago, I turned your worthless straw into gold. Now I demand what you owe me."

"Guards!" the King ordered. Ten guards rushed forward.

Rumpelstiltskin pointed his walking stick at them and muttered some words. There was a sudden flash and eight guards disappeared. Only their hats remained.

"By tomorrow you will see that the only way to save your kingdom is to give me the boy," the little man cackled, and then he was gone.

The celebration continued,
but no one laughed or smiled.
Even Peter's puppy seemed to
know that something was wrong.

That night strange things happened.

The baker woke to find hundreds
of mice in his flour bins.

A milkmaid found only four cows where there should have been twenty.

All across the kingdom farm animals had disappeared, while insects and other pests had appeared in great numbers.

News of the strange events made their way to the castle.

"What should we do?" the King asked his advisors.

Before they could answer, Rumpelstiltskin appeared. He slyly
pointed his stick at a castle wall. "Stones times one third,"
he said. The wall was suddenly full of holes. "Give me the boy,
or I will do worse."

"Leave at once!" the King demanded.

Rumpelstiltskin pointed at the King. "Nose times six," he said.

9

"It can't be!" the King spluttered. It couldn't be, it shouldn't be, but it was. The King had six noses!

Rumpelstiltskin warned, "Everyone here will have six noses if the boy doesn't come with me."

Peter said, "I will go with you, if you fix my father's nose and put everything back the way it was."

"I will," Rumpelstiltskin replied.

"No, wait!" the Queen cried, but it was too late. Peter and Rumpelstiltskin were gone.

Peter found himself standing in front of a crooked hut.
"Will you fix my father's nose now?" he asked.

"Ah!" the little man replied. "I never said I would do it right away.
First you must work to repay what your family owes me."

Rumpelstiltskin went into the hut and lit a candle. Peter saw shadowy creatures scurry into the corners. The flame barely cut through the darkness.

Rumpelstiltskin pointed his walking stick at the candle and said, "Candle times eight." The glow of eight candles brightened the room.

"How did you do that?" Peter asked.

"That is no concern of yours," the little man said. "Now go gather some firewood."

Peter collected an armful of dry wood from the surrounding forest. Rumpelstiltskin put four branches in the fireplace.

"Branches times ten," he said pointing his walking stick. He made a fire with the forty branches that appeared.

In the firelight, Peter spotted two tiny meat pies. His stomach rumbled.

Rumpelstiltskin pointed his stick at the pies and said, "Pies times five."

Ten pies appeared on the table.

Rumpelstiltskin gobbled six of the pies as Peter watched.

Peter reached for a pie and felt the stick thump the back of his hand.

"I'm saving those for later," Rumpelstiltskin said. "Now sweep the floor, and do it quietly. I'm going to sleep."

Soon, the sound of snoring filled the room.

Peter swept the floor, inching closer
and closer to the small bed.

When he was right next to the bed,
Peter gently tried to slide the stick
from the sleeping man's grasp.
It wouldn't budge.

Peter plucked a feather from Rumpelstiltskin's cap and flicked it under the sleeping man's nose.

Rumpelstiltskin let go of the stick to brush the feather away. Peter grabbed the stick and put the broom in its place.

Peter looked at the walking stick. "How does he use this?" he thought. As if in answer, Peter's stomach growled with hunger. He pointed the stick at the four pies and whispered, "Pies times five."

Nothing happened.

He tried again, this time mimicking Rumpelstiltskin's squeaky voice. The four pies just sat there.

Then he tried waving the stick like Rumpelstiltskin did. Still, the number of pies did not change.

Peter examined the stick carefully. "This X carved into the end might mean something."

He pointed the X at the pies and said, "Pies times five."

Twenty pies appeared.

"It worked!" Peter whispered. He quickly ate eight pies and could not eat anymore. "If Rumpelstiltskin sees all of these pies, he'll know I used his stick."

"There are twelve pies," Peter thought, "but there should only be four. Four pies is one-third of twelve."

Peter pointed the stick. "Pies times one-third," he said. Instantly the twelve pies became four. "Yes!" Peter exclaimed. "Maybe now I can fix my father's nose and all the other awful things Rumpelstiltskin has done."

"If I can get to the castle and back before Rumpelstiltskin wakes up, he won't even know I was gone," Peter thought, "but just in case…"

He put two chairs in front of Rumpelstiltskin's bed. "Chairs times fifty," he said pointing the stick. A wall of 100 chairs blocked the bed.

Peter backed out the hut and ran into the forest.

The sun was rising as Peter headed for the castle. On the way, he heard a voice calling, "Help! Someone, please help me."

Running toward the voice, Peter saw a boy standing on a stone in the middle of a river.

"Help!" the boy cried. "Yesterday I was walking across the river when most of the stones disappeared. I've been stuck here all night."

Peter knew it was Rumpelstiltskin's work.

"How many stepping stones were here before?" he asked.

"Twenty-seven," the boy said. "I count them every day as
I walk across. Now there are only three stones left."

Peter picked up twenty-seven pebbles and put them down
in groups of three. Then he pointed the walking stick and
said, "Stepping stones times nine."

The boy whooped with joy as he crossed the river. Peter
waved goodbye before hurrying on to the castle.

Along the way, Peter ran into more of Rumpelstiltskin's mischief.

He multiplied by twelve to help a family who had lost all but two of their chickens.

He multiplied by one-thirtieth to help a seamstress whose spools were full of spiders.

Soon Peter could see the castle in the distance. He ran faster.

As he neared the castle, Peter heard a strange buzzing.
Grasshoppers were chewing on every plant in the royal garden.

The gardener wailed as the bugs attacked the tender, green leaves.

Peter pointed the walking stick at the garden. "Grasshoppers
times one one-hundredth," he said.

"Thank you," the gardener sobbed. "A few more minutes
and there would have been nothing left."

Peter hurried from the garden into the castle.

"You got away from that horrible man!" the Queen cried in relief.

Peter hugged his parents and explained, "I don't have much time. I have to get back before Rumpelstiltskin knows I'm gone."

Peter pointed the walking stick at his father and said, "Nose times one-sixth."

"Thank goodness," the King said sniffing deeply. "My royal nose is restored to its normal number. Now every sneeze won't be such an ordeal."

Peter was about to fix the castle walls when he heard
a thundering boom and saw a cloud of smoke.

"Thought you could get away, did you?" Rumpelstiltskin scoffed.

Peter raised the walking stick. "Rumpelstiltskin times none!"
he shouted. Nothing happened.

"That's not how it works," the little man
cackled as he grabbed the stick.

Peter held on to the stick with all his might and shouted, "Rumpelstiltskin times nothing!" The little man was still there, and surprisingly strong. Peter was losing his grip. He made one last try. "Rumpelstiltskin times zero!"

A flash of lightning made Peter close his eyes. When he looked again, Rumpelstiltskin was gone.

That night the whole kingdom celebrated. Peter fixed all the bad things Rumpelstiltskin had done. Peter multiplied by whole numbers to bring back the people, animals, and objects that had disappeared. He multiplied by fractions to get rid of all of the extra insects and other pests.

When everything was the way it should be, Peter hid the stick where no one would find it.

As the story of Peter's bravery spread, children began playing a new game based on his adventure.

Times a whole will make you many;
Times a fraction leaves hardly any.
Times a zero will leave no one;
Multiplying Menace is on the run.

Multiplying is a fast way of counting groups or sets. If you multiply 4 times 5, you will get 20 faster than if you counted. So why does multiplying by a fraction make a smaller number? Because a fraction describes a piece. $\frac{1}{5}$ =

The top number tells you how many pieces you have and the bottom number tells you how many pieces make up the whole. Multiplying by a fraction is a fast way of counting pieces.

When you read, watch for the multiplication signal words: *times* and *of*.

Ten *times* six is sixty. (10 x 6 = 60)

One third *of* nine is three. ($\frac{1}{3}$ x 9 = 3)

7